NOTE TO PARENTS

Learning to read is an important skill for all children. It is a big milestone that you can help your child reach. The American Museum of Natural History Easy Reader program is designed to support you and your child through this process. Developed by reading specialists, each book in the series includes carefully selected words and sentence structures to help children advance from beginner to intermediate to proficient readers.

Here are some tips to keep in mind as you read these books with your child:

First, preview the book together. Read the title. Then look at the cover. Ask your child, "What is happening on the cover? What do you think this book is about?"

Next, skim through the pages of the book and look at the illustrations. This will help your child use the illustrations to understand the story.

Then encourage your child to read. If he or she stumbles over words, try some of these strategies:

- **use the pictures as clues**
- **point out words that are repeated**
- **sound out difficult words**
- **break up bigger words into smaller chunks**
- **use the context to lend meaning**

Finally, find out if your child understands what he or she is reading. After you have finished reading, ask, "What happened in this book?"

Above all, understand that each child learns to read at a different rate. Make sure to praise your young reader and provide encouragement along the way!

LEVEL 1

Introduce Your Child to Reading
Simple words and simple sentences encourage beginning readers to sound out words.

LEVEL 2

Your Child Starts to Read
Slightly more difficult words in simple sentences help new readers build confidence.

LEVEL 3

Your Child Reads with Help
More complex words and sentences and longer text lengths help young readers reach reading proficiency.

LEVEL 4

Your Child Reads Alone
Practicing difficult words and sentences brings independent readers to the next level: reading chapter books.

For Hank
—K.K.

STERLING CHILDREN'S BOOKS
New York

An Imprint of Sterling Publishing
387 Park Avenue South
New York, NY 10016

STERLING CHILDREN'S BOOKS and the distinctive Sterling Children's Books logo
are trademarks of Sterling Publishing Co., Inc.

ISBN 978-1-4027-8561-0 (hardcover)
ISBN 978-1-4027-7782-0 (paperback)

Distributed in Canada by Sterling Publishing
C/o Canadian Manda Group, 165 Dufferin Street
Toronto, Ontario, Canada M6K 3H6
Distributed in the United Kingdom by GMC Distribution Services
Castle Place, 166 High Street, Lewes, East Sussex, England BN7 1XU
Distributed in Australia by Capricorn Link (Australia) Pty. Ltd.
P.O. Box 704, Windsor, NSW 2756, Australia

For information about custom editions, special sales, and premium and corporate purchases,
please contact Sterling Special Sales at 800-805-5489 or specialsales@sterlingpublishing.com.

Printed in China
Lot #:
2   4   6   8   10   9   7   5   3
10/12

www.sterlingpublishing.com/kids

Illustrations by Julius Csotonyi
Designed by Amy Wahlfield

AMERICAN MUSEUM
OF NATURAL HISTORY

EASY READERS

DINOSAUR PETS

Kathleen Kudlinski
Illustrated by Julius Csotonyi

STERLING CHILDREN'S BOOKS
New York

Many kinds of dinosaurs lived

a long time ago.

They walked all over the earth.

Pretend you had a pet dinosaur!

Tyrannosaurus rex was big.

It had about sixty sharp teeth.

How would you brush its teeth?

Oviraptor looked like a bird.

It made a big nest on the ground.

Could it live in your backyard?

Velociraptor was no bigger than you.

It had claws to catch food.

How would you trim its claws?

Stegosaurus had spikes on its back.

It was as long as a school bus.

Picture yourself riding it to school!

Ankylosaurus's back was covered
with hard plates.
It had a big, heavy ball at the end
of its tail.

Don't let it wag its tail in your room!

Giant *Triceratops* ate plants
all day long.
This kind of food gave it lots of gas.

Wow!

This *Triceratops* makes a stinker!

Coelophysis had long, thin bones.

It ran fast.

Is your pet faster than a race car?

Protoceratops had a crown on its head.

The crown was made of bone
and skin.

How big is your pet's crown?

Apatosaurus had a very long neck.

It ate leaves and pine needles.

Don't let it eat all the plants on your street!

Maiasasaura lived in groups.

They walked together.

Where would you walk your pet?

Stegoceras had a bony head.

It may have bumped its head

into other dinosaurs.

Wear a helmet when you play
with your pet!

Microraptor was the size of

a very small chicken.

It may have moved through the air

with feathered wings.

Would you let it fly inside your house?

Which dinosaur would you choose for a pet?

 *Tyrannosaurus rex*

 *Oviraptor*

 *Velociraptor*

 *Stegosaurus*

 *Ankylosaurus*

 *Triceratops*

 *Coelophysis*

 *Protoceratops*

 *Apatosaurus*

 *Maiasaura*

 *Stegoceras*

 *Microraptor*

Can't decide?

It is hard to choose just one!

MEET THE EXPERT!

My name is **Mark Norell**. I am the chairman of the Paleontology Division at the American Museum of Natural History. I am in charge of museum collections and staff for my department. My research is on the fossils of reptiles, amphibians, and birds, and I specialize in the biology and evolution of dinosaurs. Our museum has one of the largest dinosaur collections in the world.

People often ask me what I do all day long. They also want to know how I trained for this position. My job is just like being a professor in a university. I earned a PhD and have done much research in my area. My job has four main parts. The first part is managing the day-to-day activities of the paleontology division. The second part of my job is developing museum exhibitions. This takes a lot of time, but I love that I am able to share my special knowledge with the public—which is why I also enjoy working on books like this! The third part of my job is managing a large research group that includes students, interns, technicians, artists, and photographers.

And the last part of my job is my own research: I spend several months a year traveling to places in the world where I can study and dig up dinosaur fossils. These days, I travel mostly to the Gobi Desert in Mongolia and to China, where we have made huge discoveries. We found fossil embryos from meat-eating dinosaurs, discovered some of the earliest modern birds, found and named many new kinds of dinosaurs, and even dug up well-preserved dinosaur eggs. We have been very successful, but there is still so much more to learn about dinosaurs. I will keep researching and learning for as long as I have this wonderful job. And you should keep learning all you can about dinosaurs, too!

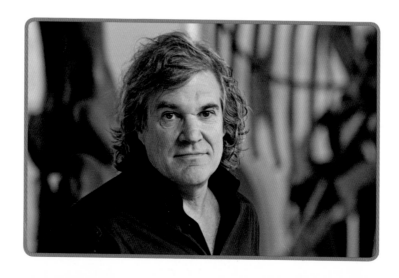

The **American Museum of Natural History** in New York City is one of the largest and most respected museums in the world. Since the Museum was founded in 1869, its collections have grown to include more than 32 million specimens and artifacts relating to the natural world and human cultures. The Museum showcases its collections in 46 exhibition halls, and behind the scenes a scientific staff of more than 200 carries out cutting-edge research. Millions of people from around the world visit the Museum each year. Plan a trip to the Museum, home of the world's largest collection of dinosaur fossils, or visit online at amnh.org.